JOY DAVIES

Pasta

JOY DAVIES

Pasta

Photography by Simon Wheeler

WEIDENFELD & NICOLSON

Joy Davies

Joy Davies began her career in food as principal researcher on *The Good Cook* series for Time-Life books. She has been cookery editor of *Woman* magazine, and was part of the team that created the *BBC Good Food* magazine. She has also been food editor of *She* and *Options* magazines, and has contributed to a number of other publications, including the *Guardian*, the *Daily Telegraph* and *Harpers & Queen*, for which she won the 1992 Glenfiddich Award (Visual Category).

Joy has travelled throughout Asia, exploring the markets, kitchens and cooking styles of India, China, Japan, Korea, Thailand, Burma and Indonesia. She lives in London.

Contents

When you walk, just walk;

when you eat, just eat.

BUDDHIST WISDOM

Introduction

How do you make pasta into a feast? Take good ingredients, treat them simply and cook with love. The recipes that follow have been chosen with this spirit in mind. The result is food that is intense, immediate and powerful. Food that has real flavour.

I am a committed olive oil cook, so all the recipes start with a good extra virgin olive oil which forms the basis of the sauce. From here you have infinite choices: add flavoursome tomatoes and simmer to a rich, sweet, fruity sauce; frazzle artichokes with bacon; wilt a handful of peppery rocket leaves; or soften thin slices of mushroom. A dash of white wine or balsamic vinegar, or a splash of chicken stock, highlights flavour and gives depth to sauces. Fresh soft-leaved herbs such as flat-leaf parsley, chervil and basil can be added at the last minute for a final aromatic burst.

With a little care, it is so simple to elevate pasta from ordinary to special. I hope these recipes inspire you to look at pasta with new eyes.

PASTA IN BRODO
Pasta in chicken broth

SERVES 4

1.5–1.8 kg/3–4 lb free-range
 chicken
1 carrot, halved
1 onion, halved
few sprigs of thyme
few sprigs of parsley
1 bay leaf
3 strips of lemon zest
6 black peppercorns
salt
125 g/4 oz dried farfalline, stelle
 or other soup pasta

To serve
fresh chervil leaves
freshly ground black pepper
freshly grated Parmesan cheese

Pull away any fat from just inside the chicken. Remove the legs, thighs and breasts. Separate the ribs from the back and chop into large pieces. Put the chicken bones and meat into a large, heavy-bottomed saucepan with the carrot and onion. Cover with cold water and bring slowly to the boil. Skim off any scum that rises to the surface. Add a few tablespoons of cold water to encourage more scum to be released. Skim every few minutes until no more scum appears, then add the herbs, lemon zest and peppercorns. Partially cover the pan and simmer for 3 hours, topping up with boiling water.

When the chicken meat is tasteless, the stock is ready. Strain into a jug or bowl, discarding the chicken and aromatics, then pour through a fine sieve into the cleaned pan. Bring the stock back to the boil and reduce to 1.5 litres/2½ pints. Add salt to taste.

To serve, add the pasta to the boiling stock and simmer until cooked, about 5–6 minutes. Serve in soup dishes, sprinkled with chervil, freshly ground black pepper and Parmesan.

For a main course, serve roast chicken with some sautéed wild and cultivated mushrooms.

PASTA E FAGIOLI
Pasta and bean soup

150 g/5 oz dried borlotti beans,
  soaked overnight in cold
  water
5 tablespoons extra virgin
  olive oil
1 cm/½ inch thick slice of
  pancetta, cut into lardons
2 sticks of celery, chopped
2 carrots, chopped
2 onions, chopped
4 tomatoes, seeded and finely
  chopped
2 sprigs of thyme
1 bay leaf
125 g/4 oz macaroni

To serve
salt and freshly ground black
  pepper
Parmesan cheese
extra virgin olive oil

Drain the soaked beans and rinse thoroughly.

Heat the olive oil in a frying pan, add the pancetta and sauté until golden. Remove the pancetta with a slotted spoon and add the celery, carrots and onions. Sauté for 5 minutes or until softened.

Put the drained beans, pancetta and vegetables, with the tomatoes, in a large, heavy-bottomed saucepan. Add the herbs and cover with water. Bring to the boil and boil rapidly for 10 minutes. Reduce the heat, partially cover the pan and simmer very gently for about 2 hours. At the end of this time the beans should be tender. If the soup becomes too dry, top up with boiling water.

Remove two-thirds of the soup and pass through a mouli-légumes or blend in a liquidizer. Return the purée to the soup, add some boiling water and bring back to the boil. Add the macaroni and simmer until tender, about 10 minutes, stirring well to prevent the pasta from sticking. Leave to stand for 10 minutes.

Serve in soup dishes, with salt and black pepper, shavings of Parmesan and a swirl of your best olive oil, accompanied by some ciabatta or other good Italian bread, lightly toasted and rubbed with a cut garlic clove and a dribble of olive oil.

Follow with another classic Venetian dish, fegato alla Veneziana: fine slices of calves' liver fried with thinly sliced onions. A salad of slightly bitter green leaves, such as curly endive, would be a good finale.

PAPPARDELLE CON FUNGHI
Pappardelle with mushrooms

SERVES 4

200 g/7 oz fresh mixed wild
  mushrooms (e.g.
  porcini/ceps, chanterelles)
  or 175 g/6 oz brown cap
  mushrooms and 15 g/½ oz
  dried porcini
4 tablespoons extra virgin
  olive oil
1 onion, finely chopped
2 garlic cloves, chopped
125 ml/4 fl oz chicken stock
1 glass of dry white wine or dry
  vermouth
225 g/8 oz dried pappardelle
1 teaspoon balsamic vinegar
2 tablespoons finely chopped
  flat-leaf parsley
salt and pepper

To serve
freshly grated Parmesan cheese

Brush any soil from the mushrooms and wipe with a damp cloth. Finely slice the porcini or brown caps, keep small chanterelles whole and cut larger ones in half. If using dried mushrooms, rinse them under a running tap, then soak in warm water for 20 minutes. Remove from the soaking liquid, reserving the liquid, and roughly chop. Carefully strain the liquid, leaving behind any gritty deposits.

Heat the olive oil in a wide saucepan, add the onion and sauté for 5 minutes. Add the garlic and sauté for a further 2 minutes; do not let the garlic colour. Add the porcini or brown cap mushrooms and sauté for 5 minutes.

If using only fresh mushrooms, add the more delicate mushrooms and cook for a further 3 minutes. Add the stock and wine, bring to the boil, then simmer to reduce to a light coating consistency.

Alternatively, add the soaked dried mushrooms, soaking liquid, stock, wine and 100 ml/3½ fl oz water to the sautéed brown caps. Simmer, covered, for 20 minutes or until the dried mushrooms are tender.

To serve, cook the pasta (page 35). Sprinkle the balsamic vinegar over the mushrooms. Heat through for a couple of minutes, then add the parsley and season to taste. Toss with the cooked, drained pasta and serve with Parmesan.

Follow with grilled spatchcocked quail that has been marinated with garlic, lemon zest, chilli and herbs, or roast guinea fowl.

LINGUINE PRIMAVERA
Linguine with spring vegetables

SERVES 4

3 tablespoons extra virgin
   olive oil
1 garlic clove, chopped
150 g/5 oz dried linguine
3 carrots, shredded
125 g/4 oz fine green beans,
   topped and tailed, halved
   lengthwise if thick
3 courgettes, shredded
1 tablespoon pesto sauce
½ lemon
salt and pepper

To serve
freshly grated Parmesan cheese

Heat the olive oil in a saucepan, add the garlic and sauté for 1 minute. Discard the garlic.

Cook the pasta (page 35). Steam the carrots for 2 minutes. Add the beans and steam for a further 2 minutes. Add the courgettes and cook for 1 minute.

Mix the pesto with the garlic-infused oil, a generous squeeze of lemon juice, salt and pepper. Add the hot vegetables and stir to coat. Add the cooked, drained pasta and toss well. Serve with Parmesan.

Follow with fresh prawns sautéed in olive oil with garlic and parsley.

CASARECCIA AL POMODORO
Casareccia with tomato sauce

SERVES 4

1.5 kg/3 lb good-flavoured vine-
ripened tomatoes
6 tablespoons extra virgin olive
oil
225 g/8 oz dried casareccia or
penne rigate
salt and pepper

To serve
Parmesan cheese

Halve the tomatoes, scoop out the seeds, cut away and
discard any tough cores and chop the flesh finely.

Heat half the olive oil in a heavy-bottomed saucepan.
Add the tomatoes and simmer for 30 minutes, shaking
the pan occasionally to release the moisture from the
tomatoes. Add the remaining oil from time to time.

Meanwhile, cook the pasta (page 35). The sauce is ready
when the oil separates from the tomato pulp. Season to
taste, add the cooked, drained pasta and toss well. Serve
with shavings of Parmesan.

*To serve as a light lunch or supper, begin with a selection of
Italian salami.*

RAVIOLI CON UOVO DI QUAGLIE
Ravioli with quails' eggs

SERVES 4

4 lasagne sheets
1–2 tablespoons flour
85 g/3 oz Fontina cheese, cut
    into strips
4 quails' eggs
salt and pepper
handful of fresh chervil

To serve
extra virgin olive oil
freshly grated Parmesan cheese

Boil the lasagne, two sheets at a time, for 9 minutes. Refresh in cold water and leave to dry on a clean tea towel. Rub the lasagne sheets with a little flour, then cut each sheet in half to make two squares.

Using four strips of cheese, form a square in the centre of half the pasta squares. Crack a quails' egg into the centre of the cheese squares. Season with salt and pepper and sprinkle on some chervil. Top with another pasta square and press firmly to seal the edges. Trim with a fluted pastry wheel.

Gently lower into a wide saucepan of simmering water and simmer for 1 minute. Drain and serve sprinkled with chervil, extra virgin olive oil, salt, freshly ground black pepper and Parmesan.

Follow with grilled salmon, and fresh spinach wilted briefly in a pan with some olive oil and dressed with lemon juice.

TAGLIARDI CON CARCIOFINI
Tagliardi with baby artichokes and pancetta

SERVES 4

12 baby artichokes
1 lemon
4 tablespoons extra virgin
   olive oil
2 onions, sliced
2 slices of pancetta, about
   1 cm/½ inch thick, cut into
   lardons
2 glasses of dry white wine
225 g/8 oz dried tagliardi
salt and pepper

To serve
freshly grated Parmesan cheese

Break off any short stalks from the artichokes and then pull away the tough outer leaves until the tender yellow leaves are visible. Trim the bases and cut off the top 1–2.5 cm/½–1 inch of the leaves. Quarter or cut into six, depending on size, and toss into a large bowl of cold water, to which you have added the juice of the lemon.

Heat the olive oil in a large sauté pan, add the onions and pancetta and sauté for 5 minutes. Add the artichokes and cook, stirring occasionally, for about 20 minutes, until the artichokes are golden and tender. Add the wine and cook over a high heat to reduce to a syrupy glaze.

Meanwhile, cook the pasta (page 35). Add the cooked, drained pasta to the artichokes and toss well. Season to taste and serve with Parmesan.

Follow with roast lamb cooked with fresh rosemary or thyme, with whole, unpeeled garlic cloves added to the roasting dish for the final 40 minutes.

FETTUCELLE CON BOTTARGA
Fettucelle with bottarga and rocket

SERVES 4

225 g/8 oz dried fettucelle
4 tablespoons extra virgin
  olive oil
125 g/4 oz fresh rocket (arugula)
2 tablespoons grated bottarga,
  plus extra, to serve

To serve
freshly ground black pepper
lemon halves
freshly grated Parmesan cheese

Cook the pasta (page 35).

Heat the olive oil in a saucepan, add the rocket and toss for 1 minute or until wilted. Add to the cooked, drained pasta, sprinkle with 2 tablespoons of bottarga and toss well. Season with black pepper and serve with lemon halves, Parmesan, and extra bottarga at the table.

Follow with grilled fresh tuna that has been briefly marinated with lemon, garlic, a little chilli, fresh herbs and olive oil, accompanied by a tomato salad.

SPAGHETTINI CON AGLIO E OLIO
Spaghettini with garlic, oil and chilli

SERVES 4

4 tablespoons extra virgin
  olive oil
12 garlic cloves, thinly sliced
4 dried red chillies, seeds
  removed, chopped
225 g/8 oz dried spaghettini
salt and pepper

Heat the olive oil over a gentle heat, add the garlic and cook gently until tender and lightly coloured. Add the chillies and cook for a further minute. Leave to stand while you cook the pasta (page 35).

Add the cooked, drained pasta to the garlic-infused oil. Toss well and season with salt and freshly ground black pepper. This should not be served with Parmesan.

Follow with chargrilled squid and mixed grilled vegetables.

TAGLIARDI CON TOTANI E CIPOLLA
Tagliardi with baby squid and spring onions

SERVES 4

12 baby squid
8 large spring onions, trimmed
3–4 tablespoons extra virgin
   olive oil
225 g/8 oz dried spinach
   tagliardi
3 garlic cloves, chopped
4 tomatoes, seeded and finely
   chopped
1 tablespoon chopped fresh
   parsley
1 small red chilli, seeded, ribs
   removed and finely chopped
salt and pepper

To serve

lemon halves

Pull the squid tentacles away from the bodies and cut off the tentacles just below the eyes. Feel around the body tube for the transparent backbone and remove. Rub the purple skin from the tubes, then cut the tubes into rings.

Brush the spring onions with olive oil and grill or griddle for 2–3 minutes on each side until golden, tender and slightly charred. Cut each one into three pieces.

Cook the pasta (page 35). Meanwhile, heat 2 table-spoons of the oil in a sauté pan, add the garlic and sauté for 2 minutes. Add the squid and cook over a high heat for 3 minutes. Add the tomatoes, spring onions, parsley and chilli and stir to combine. Toss with the cooked, drained pasta, season with salt and freshly ground black pepper and serve with lemon halves. This should not be served with Parmesan.

Precede or follow with a platter of grilled aubergines and mixed peppers.

TAGLIATELLE CON SALMONE E CAVIAR
Tagliatelle with fresh salmon, caviar and truffle

SERVES 4

125 g/4 oz dried tagliatelle
175 g/6 oz fresh salmon fillet
2–3 tablespoons extra virgin
olive oil
sea salt and freshly ground black
pepper
25 g/1 oz caviar
few slices of white or black
truffle (optional), or substitute
1–2 teaspoons truffle oil for
some of the olive oil

Cook the pasta (page 35).

Skin and thinly slice the salmon. Drain the pasta, add the salmon and stir to cook in the heat. Add the olive oil, salt and pepper and toss well.

Serve at once on individual plates, topped with a teaspoonful of caviar and a couple of thin shavings from the truffle. This should not be served with Parmesan.

A very luxurious, elegant starter, which could be followed with grilled asparagus accompanied by boiled quails' eggs and prosciutto.

TAGLIATELLE CON SARDE IN SAOR
Tagliatelle with marinated sardines

SERVES 6

4 tablespoons extra virgin
   olive oil
3 onions, thinly sliced
2 bay leaves
3 tablespoons white wine vinegar
1 teaspoon black peppercorns
1 tablespoon raisins, plumped
   for 15 minutes in hot water
8 fresh sardines, scaled,
   cleaned, heads removed
plain flour for dredging
salt and pepper
275 g/10 oz dried tagliatelle

To serve
lemon halves

Heat 3 tablespoons of the olive oil in a saucepan over a low heat and gently cook the onions with the bay leaves until tender and starting to colour, about 20 minutes. Add the vinegar, peppercorns and raisins and stir to mix.

Rinse the sardines well under running water, cleaning out any blood from near the bone. Dry thoroughly on paper towels. Heat the remaining oil in a frying pan. Dredge the sardines in seasoned flour and fry a few at a time for 2 minutes on each side until golden. Drain on paper towels.

Put half the onion mixture into a dish large enough to hold the sardines in a single layer. Season with salt and pepper. Top with the sardines and the remaining onion mixture. Cover and leave to marinate in a cool place (not the refrigerator) for 10 hours, turning after 5 hours.

Cook the pasta (page 35) and fillet the sardines, keeping the tails intact. Heat the onion mixture through gently, add the sardines and the cooked pasta and toss for 1 minute. Season with freshly ground black pepper and serve with lemon halves.

I would be tempted to follow this robust dish with a selection of steamed or chargrilled vegetables tossed with olive oil and lemon juice and flakes of fresh Parmesan. Perhaps new potatoes (Jersey royals if in season), fresh peas, broad beans, baby artichokes or quartered artichoke bottoms.

The Basics

CHOOSING PASTA

There is a common misconception that fresh pasta is better than dried. I believe the reverse is true. The best pasta is made from 100% durum (hard) wheat, *grano duro*. Italian manufacturers have to comply with this by law; packets will declare *pasta di semola de grano duro*. I can recommend the following brands: Cipriani, Agnesi, De Cecco, Martelli and Voiello.

SHAPES

There are some simple guidelines as to which pasta to marry with which sauce. Long thin strands such as spaghetti and spaghettini work well with light dressings and sauces based on olive oil. Spaghettini is traditional with seafood. Thicker ribbons of tagliatelle or even thicker fettucine are best with thicker sauces, especially cream-based ones. Meat sauces work well with shapes, for example fusilli, as the spirals trap plenty of sauce. When serving green sauces, such as pesto, provide contrast with plain egg pasta; spinach pasta would mask the brilliant green colour of the sauce.

Beware of some shapes which do not cook evenly, such as farfalle (butterflies); I always find that the centre is still hard when the outer edge is cooked.

QUANTITIES

The structure of lunch or dinner in Italy is different to that in Britain. Pasta is served after an appetizer or antipasti and before the main dish. Served in this way, allow 50 g/2 oz dried pasta per person (double the quantity if using fresh pasta). If you do choose to serve pasta as a main dish, allow 85 g/3 oz per person.

Cooking pasta

Pasta needs to be cooked in a large amount of salted water in a big pot, so that the starch from the pasta is well diluted in the water and does not become gluey. Allow 1 litre/1¾ pints water per 100 g/4 oz pasta, bring the water to the boil, then add 1 teaspoon sea salt per litre. Allow the water to come back to a full rolling boil before adding the pasta, all at once. Push long strands under the water and stir well with a fork to separate. Cover with a lid so that the water returns to the boil quickly. I usually add a dash of olive oil to the water to help keep the pasta separate.

The cooking time depends on the size, shape and dryness of the pasta. Some very fine pasta cooks in 2 minutes, other varieties may take 12 minutes. Use the packet instructions as a rough guide and start testing a few minutes before the time is up. The term 'al dente', means that the pasta should have a bite to it but not a hard core. Timing is critical, so test every 30 seconds. by removing one piece and biting it. Once cooked, drain the pasta into a colander immediately, otherwise it will overcook. Some chefs add a cupful of cold water to the pot to arrest cooking.

Give the colander two or three good shakes and toss the pasta with a little olive oil and a couple of tablespoons of freshly grated Parmesan cheese, if using. Add the pasta to the sauce and toss quickly and lightly with two forks. Pasta does not need to be completely dry before tossing with the sauce; in fact, you can keep a cup of the cooking water on hand and add it to the sauce to help it coat the pasta better. Transfer to a heated serving dish or serve straight into soup plates.

ESSENTIAL INGREDIENTS

SALT

Use a good-quality sea salt. I like the salt that comes in flaky crystals, crumbled directly on to the dish.

BLACK PEPPER

The Italian restaurant custom of bringing a pepper grinder to the table is, despite the jokes, based on good sense. Black pepper is aromatic, and should be used as a final seasoning, as its essential aroma and flavour are lost in cooking. Ready-ground black pepper has also lost its aroma; what is left is mere pungency.

OLIVE OIL

I always use extra virgin olive oil in cooking, choosing a modest quality for frying and a finer, estate-bottled oil when I need small quantities as a seasoning. Buy the best you can afford and the taste you prefer.

PARMESAN CHEESE

Freshly grated Parmesan cheese is essential to many pasta dishes, although it is never served with clams. It is made in northern Italy, in and around the province of Parma, and its rind is stamped 'Parmigiano Reggiano'. Before it can be sold it must be aged for at least one year. It has a buttery yellow colour and a mellow, nutty, slightly salty flavour. Ask to taste Parmesan before you buy it. Once grated, the cheese quickly loses its flavour. Never buy ready-grated Parmesan in tubs or jars: the unpleasant-smelling granules will put you off for life.

Once cut, Parmesan soon dries out. Store tightly wrapped in waxed or greaseproof paper then in a layer of foil. After a week or so, as the cheese dries it may develop a whitish bloom. Wrap in damp muslin and then foil and refrigerate overnight. Remove the muslin the following day and rewrap. Parmesan will keep for a few weeks in the refrigerator. I am told it also freezes well.

GRANA PADANO CHEESE	Grana Padano is a Parmesan lookalike made outside the area restricted to true Parmesan. It has none of the depth of flavour of Parmesan and, although perfectly fine as a table cheese, bears no comparison to Parmesan in cooking.
PANCETTA	Italian belly pork (the same cut as streaky bacon) cured with salt and spices, and sold smoked or unsmoked. For cooking, buy pancetta in a flat piece, with its rind attached. Cut into thick rashers, then cut across into chunky strips, or lardons. Store tightly wrapped in the refrigerator.
BALSAMIC VINEGAR	Good-quality balsamic vinegar is very expensive. It is produced exclusively in Modena and aged for a number of years in wooden casks. Only the genuine article can be labelled Aceto Balsamico Tradizionale di Modena. It is darker and thicker than regular vinegar and has a complex sweet and sharp flavour. It should be used by the drop, not the spoonful.
BOTTARGA	Grey mullet roe, salted, pressed and sun-dried. A speciality of Sardinia, bottarga has a very savoury, fishy, sweet-salt flavour. To use, peel away the membrane and grate finely over pasta. It is sold whole or ready-grated from Italian shops.
PORCINI SECCHI	Dried porcini mushrooms (ceps, or *boletus edulis*) should have a potent aroma that almost knocks you over. They are a miracle ingredient in pasta sauces, particularly good with meat. They are sold either in large, creamy-coloured, mushroom-shaped slices, or in smaller chips. The former command a high price and are considered to have the best flavour, but the smaller pieces are good as an additional ingredient.

Classic Cooking

STARTERS

Jean Christophe Novelli Chef/patron of Maison Novelli, which opened in London to great acclaim in 1996. He previously worked at the Four Seasons restaurant, London.

VEGETABLE SOUPS

Elisabeth Luard Cookery writer for the *Sunday Telegraph Magazine* and author of *European Peasant Food* and *European Festival Food*, which won a Glenfiddich Award.

GOURMET SALADS

Sonia Stevenson The first woman chef in the UK to be awarded a Michelin star, at the Horn of Plenty in Devon. Author of *The Magic of Saucery* and *Fresh Ways with Fish*.

FISH AND SHELLFISH

Gordon Ramsay Chef/proprietor of one of London's most popular restaurants, Aubergine, recently awarded its second Michelin star. He is the author of *A Passion for Flavour*.

CHICKEN, DUCK AND GAME

Nick Nairn Chef/patron of Braeval restaurant near Aberfoyle in Scotland, whose BBC-TV series *Wild Harvest* was last summer's most successful cookery series, accompanied by a book.

LIVERS, SWEETBREADS AND KIDNEYS

Simon Hopkinson Former chef/patron at London's Bibendum restaurant, columnist and author of *Roast Chicken and Other Stories* and the forthcoming *The Prawn Cocktail Years*.

VEGETARIAN

Rosamond Richardson Author of several vegetarian titles, including *The Great Green Gourmet* and *Food from Green Places*. She has also appeared on television.

PASTA

Joy Davies One of the creators of *BBC Good Food Magazine*, she has been food editor of *She, Woman* and *Options* and written for the *Guardian, Daily Telegraph* and *Harpers & Queen*.

CHEESE DISHES

Rose Elliot The UK's most successful vegetarian cookery writer and author of many books, including *Not Just a Load of Old Lentils* and *The Classic Vegetarian Cookbook*.

POTATO DISHES

Patrick McDonald Author of the forthcoming *Simply Good Food* and Harvey Nichols' food consultant.

BISTRO COOKING

Anne Willan Founder and director of La Varenne Cookery School in Burgundy and West Virginia. Author of many books and a specialist in French cuisine.

ITALIAN COOKING

Anna Del Conte is the author of *The Classic Food of Northern Italy* (chosen as the 1996 Guild of Food Writers Book of the Year) and *The Gastronomy of Italy*. She has appeared on BBC-TV's *Masterchef*.

VIETNAMESE COOKING

Nicole Routhier One of the United States' most popular cookery writers, her books include *Cooking Under Wraps, Nicole Routhier's Fruit Cookbook* and the award-winning *The Foods of Vietnam*.

MALAYSIAN COOKING

Jill Dupleix One of Australia's best known cookery writers, with columns in the *Sydney Morning Herald* and *Elle*. Author of *New Food, Allegro al dente* and the Master Chefs *Pacific*.

PEKING CUISINE

Helen Chen Learned to cook traditional Peking dishes from her mother, Joyce Chen, the grande dame of Chinese cooking in the United States. The author of *Chinese Home Cooking*.

STIR FRIES

Kay Fairfax Author of several books, including *100 Great Stir-fries, Homemade* and *The Australian Christmas Book*.

NOODLES

Terry Durack Australia's most widely read restaurant critic and co-editor of the *Sydney Morning Herald Good Food Guide*. He is the author of *YUM!*, a book of stories and recipes.

NORTH INDIAN CURRIES

Pat Chapman Started the Curry Club in 1982. Appears regularly on television and radio and is the author of eighteen books, the latest being *The Thai Restaurant Cookbook*.

BARBECUES AND GRILLS

Brian Turner Chef/patron of Turner's in Knightsbridge and one of Britain's most popular food broadcasters; he appears frequently on *Ready Steady Cook, Food and Drink* and many other television programmes.

SUMMER AND WINTER CASSEROLES

Anton Edelmann Maître Chef des Cuisines at the Savoy Hotel, London, and author of six books. He appears regularly on BBC-TV's *Masterchef*.

TRADITIONAL PUDDINGS

Tessa Bramley Chef/patron of the acclaimed Old Vicarage restaurant in Ridgeway, Derbyshire. Author of *The Instinctive Cook*, and a regular presenter on a new Channel 4 daytime series *Here's One I Made Earlier*.

DECORATED CAKES

Jane Asher Author of several cookery books and a novel. She has also appeared in her own television series, *Jane Asher's Christmas* (1995).

FAVOURITE CAKES

Mary Berry One of Britain's leading cookery writers, her numerous books include *Mary Berry's Ultimate Cake Book*. She has made many television and radio appearances and is a regular contributor to cookery magazines.

Photographs © Simon Wheeler 1997

First published in 1997 by
George Weidenfeld & Nicolson
The Orion Publishing Group
Orion House
5 Upper St Martin's Lane
London WC2H 9EA

British Library Cataloguing-in-Publication data
A catalogue record for this book is available from
the British Library

ISBN 0 297 82339 6

Designed by Lucy Holmes
Edited by Maggie Ramsay
Food styling by Joy Davies
Typeset by Tiger Typeset